# TRAVEL GUIDE TO MALDIVES 2023

The Ultimate Travel Guide To Maldives; Discover what to see, what to do, where to stay, with 7-Days Itinerary Guide for first timers

**Jade Green**

All rights reserved. No part of this publication may be reproduced, distributed, or transmitted in any form or by any means, including photocopying, recording, or other electronic or mechanical methods, without the prior written permission of the publisher, except in the case of brief quotations embodied in critical reviews and certain other noncommercial uses permitted by copyright law.

Copyright © Jade Green, 2023.

Table of contents

Introduction

10 Reasons to visit Maldives

20 Top-Rated Tourist Attraction in Maldives

Maldives Travel Expenses

Backpacking Maldives Recommended Budgets

Maldives Money Saving Tips

How to Travel Around Maldives

How to be Safe in Maldives

The Maldives Tourist Visa

10 Days in Maldives

Maldives Culture; facts, customs and traditions

Maldives top Hotels

10 top Beaches in Maldives

Conclusion

# Introduction

Nestled in the heart of the Indian Ocean lies a tropical paradise like no other: the Maldives. Composed of over 1,000 coral islands, this archipelago nation boasts crystal-clear turquoise waters, pristine white sandy beaches, and an abundance of marine life that will leave you in awe. With its luxurious resorts, diverse cultural heritage, and unrivaled natural beauty, the Maldives is truly a destination that promises to captivate the hearts of travelers from all corners of the globe. Whether you're seeking a romantic honeymoon getaway, a family vacation, or an adventurous diving expedition, the Maldives is a world-class destination that will leave you with unforgettable memories that will last a lifetime.

The Maldives is a tropical paradise located in South Asia, composed of 26 atolls made up of over 1,000 coral islands. The country is known for its stunning natural beauty, with turquoise lagoons, coral reefs, and white sandy beaches that are perfect for sunbathing, swimming, and snorkeling.

With its warm and sunny climate, the Maldives is a year-round destination that offers a variety of activities for visitors to enjoy. The crystal-clear waters of the Indian Ocean are home to an array of marine life, making it a popular spot for snorkeling, scuba diving, and deep-sea fishing. Visitors can also explore the many islands and atolls by boat, kayak, or stand-up paddleboard.

In addition to its natural beauty, the Maldives has a rich cultural heritage that is influenced by Indian, Sri Lankan, and Arab traditions. Visitors can learn about the country's history and culture by visiting local museums, exploring ancient ruins, and attending traditional festivals and ceremonies.

The Maldives is also known for its luxurious resorts, which offer a range of amenities and activities such as spas, restaurants, and water sports. These resorts are located on their own private islands, providing visitors with a sense of exclusivity and privacy.

However, the best time to visit the Maldives depends on your preferences, budget, and travel plans.

The Maldives has two distinct seasons: the dry season (December to April) and the wet season (May to November). The dry season is the peak tourist season, with sunny and dry weather, calm seas, and clear waters, making it an ideal time for water activities such as snorkeling and diving. The dry season also coincides with the Christmas and New Year holidays, as well as the Chinese New Year, which means that prices for accommodation and flights are generally higher during this time.

On the other hand, the wet season in the Maldives brings more rain and stronger winds, which can affect the visibility of the water and the quality of diving and snorkeling. However, the wet season also brings lower prices and fewer crowds, making it a great time to visit if you're on a budget and prefer a quieter, more relaxed atmosphere.

If you're planning to visit the Maldives for specific activities, such as surfing, the best time to visit is between May and October when the waves are at their best. Similarly, if you're interested in seeing manta rays and whale sharks, the best time to visit is between June and November.

Dry Season:
The dry season in the Maldives is from December to April, and this is the most popular time for tourists to visit. During this season, the weather is sunny and dry, with temperatures ranging from the mid-20s to low 30s degrees Celsius. The sea is calm and clear, making it ideal for swimming, snorkeling,

and diving. The dry season is also a great time for romantic getaways, as the beaches are not crowded, and the atmosphere is serene. However, the downside of visiting during the dry season is that the prices for flights and accommodation can be significantly higher.

Wet Season:
The wet season in the Maldives is from May to November, and during this time, there is a higher chance of rain and storms. The weather is still warm, with temperatures ranging from the mid-20s to high 20s degrees Celsius. However, the sea can be rough, which can affect visibility for water activities like diving and snorkeling. Despite this, the wet season is a great time to visit the Maldives if you're on a budget, as prices for flights and accommodation are generally lower. Additionally, during this time, the Maldives experiences fewer tourists, so you can enjoy a more peaceful and less crowded atmosphere.

Other factors to consider:
If you're interested in surfing, the best time to visit the Maldives is from March to October when the waves are at their best. If you're looking to experience the Maldives' unique underwater marine life, then the best time to visit is between May and

November when manta rays and whale sharks are more likely to be seen. It's also important to note that the Maldives is a Muslim country, and Ramadan is observed during the ninth month of the Islamic calendar. During this time, some restaurants and shops may be closed, and there may be restrictions on the sale of alcohol.

Overall, the best time to visit the Maldives depends on your preferences and travel plans. If you're looking for sunny weather and calm seas for water activities, then the dry season is the ideal time to visit. However, if you're on a budget and prefer a quieter atmosphere, then the wet season may be a better option. Whatever time you choose to visit, you're sure to have an unforgettable experience in this tropical paradise.

Overall, the Maldives is a destination that has something to offer for every type of traveler. Whether you're looking to relax and unwind, explore the natural beauty of the islands, or immerse yourself in the local culture, the Maldives is a destination that promises to leave you with unforgettable memories.

## 10 Reasons to Visit Maldives

Maldives is a unique and exotic destination that offers a once-in-a-lifetime experience. From its pristine beaches and crystal-clear waters to its luxurious resorts and vibrant marine life, the Maldives is a destination that promises to captivate and delight visitors of all ages and interests. Whether you're seeking a romantic getaway, an adventure-packed vacation, or simply a relaxing escape from the stresses of everyday life, the Maldives is a destination that is sure to leave you with unforgettable memories that will last a lifetime.

**Here are 10 reasons why you should consider visiting the Maldives;**

**1. Stunning natural beauty:** The Maldives is known for its breathtaking natural beauty, with pristine beaches, crystal-clear waters, and colorful coral reefs that are teeming with marine life.

**2. Luxury resorts:** The Maldives is home to some of the most luxurious resorts in the world, offering a range of amenities such as private beaches, overwater bungalows, and world-class restaurants.

**3. Water sports:** With its warm waters and vibrant marine life, the Maldives is the perfect place to enjoy a variety of water sports such as snorkeling, scuba diving, and deep-sea fishing.

**4. Island hopping:** The Maldives is composed of over 1,000 coral islands, each with its own unique charm and character. Visitors can explore the many islands by boat, seaplane, or even by swimming between them.

**5. Romantic getaways:** The Maldives is a popular destination for honeymooners and couples looking for a romantic getaway, with its secluded beaches, private villas, and stunning sunsets.

**6. Local culture:** The Maldives has a rich cultural heritage that is influenced by Indian, Sri Lankan, and Arab traditions. Visitors can experience the local culture by attending traditional festivals and ceremonies, visiting local museums, and exploring ancient ruins.

**7. Unspoiled nature:** Despite its popularity as a tourist destination, much of the Maldives remains unspoiled and untouched. Visitors can enjoy a sense of tranquility and solitude on many of the islands.

**8. Spa treatments:** Many of the resorts in the Maldives offer world-class spa treatments that incorporate local ingredients and traditional techniques.

**9. Eco-tourism:** The Maldives is committed to preserving its natural beauty and protecting its delicate ecosystem. Visitors can learn about the country's conservation efforts and participate in eco-tourism activities such as reef cleanups and turtle conservation programs.

**10. Stunning sunsets:** The Maldives is famous for its stunning sunsets, which can be enjoyed from many of the beaches and resorts throughout the country. Watching the sun dip below the horizon is a magical experience that you won't want to miss.

## 20 Top-Rated Tourist Attraction in Maldives

Maldives is a tropical paradise located in the Indian Ocean, known for its crystal-clear waters, white-sand beaches, and exotic marine life. This island nation comprises 26 atolls and over 1,000 coral islands, offering endless opportunities for exploration and relaxation. Here are the 20 top-rated tourist attractions in the Maldives that you should add to your itinerary.

**1. Male:** The capital city of the Maldives is a vibrant hub of activity and culture, featuring historic landmarks, bustling markets, and scenic views of the ocean.

**2. Hulhumale:** A man-made island located near Male, Hulhumale is known for its pristine beaches, water sports activities, and stunning sunsets.

**3. Maafushi Island:** One of the largest islands in the Maldives, Maafushi is a popular tourist destination that offers a variety of activities, including snorkeling, scuba diving, and beach picnics.

**4. Alimatha Island:** Located in the Vaavu Atoll, Alimatha Island is known for its exotic marine life, including colorful fish, sea turtles, and even sharks.

**5. Banana Reef:** This underwater paradise is a popular spot for snorkeling and diving, thanks to its abundant coral formations and diverse marine life.

**6. Manta Point:** Home to manta rays and other sea creatures, Manta Point is a must-visit destination for underwater enthusiasts.

**7. Vabbinfaru Island:** This secluded island is known for its luxurious resorts, stunning beaches, and picturesque sunsets.

**8. Veligandu Island Beach:** Featuring crystal-clear waters and white-sand beaches, Veligandu Island Beach is a paradise for sunbathers and swimmers.

**9. Utheemu Island:** This historic island is home to a 500-year-old palace, which served as the residence of Sultan Mohamed Thakurufaanu.

**10. Biyadhoo Island:** Surrounded by a pristine coral reef, Biyadhoo Island is a popular spot for snorkeling and diving.

**11. Kuda Bandos Island:** This tiny island is known for its secluded beaches, clear waters, and abundant marine life.

**12. Fihalhohi Island:** A popular destination for honeymooners, Fihalhohi Island is known for its romantic ambiance, private villas, and stunning sunsets.

**13. Baros Island:** A luxury resort located in North Male Atoll, Baros Island is known for its overwater villas, spa treatments, and fine dining.

**14. Reethi Beach Island:** Located in the Baa Atoll, Reethi Beach Island is known for its vibrant coral gardens, lush vegetation, and serene atmosphere.

**15. Velassaru Island:** A picturesque island located in the South Male Atoll, Velassaru Island is known for its luxurious villas, private beaches, and panoramic ocean views.

**16. Dhigali Island:** Featuring a pristine beach, crystal-clear waters, and lush vegetation, Dhigali Island is a popular destination for nature lovers.

**17. Sun Island Resort & Spa:** A popular resort located in the South Ari Atoll, Sun Island Resort & Spa offers a range of activities, including diving, fishing, and island hopping.

**18. Vilamendhoo Island Resort & Spa:** This all-inclusive resort is known for its stunning beaches, crystal-clear waters, and abundant marine life.

**19. Kuramathi Island:** Featuring a variety of accommodations, including beach villas and overwater bungalows, Kuramathi Island is a popular destination for couples and families.

**20. Conrad Maldives Rangali Island:** Featuring an underwater restaurant, a luxury spa, and private villas, Conrad Maldives Rangali Island is the ultimate

## Maldives Travel Expenses

**Flights**
The cost of flights to the Maldives can vary greatly depending on your location and the time of year you plan to travel. On average, flights from the United States can range from $1,000 to $2,000 per person. If you're traveling from Europe, expect to pay anywhere from $500 to $1,500 per person.

To get the best deals on flights to the Maldives, it's recommended that you book your tickets well in advance of your travel date, as last-minute flights can be much more expensive. You can also try to travel during the off-peak season, which is generally from May to November, when prices are likely to be lower.

Additionally, consider using travel reward points or miles to offset the cost of your flights. Many airlines and credit card companies offer travel rewards programs that allow you to earn points or miles with each purchase, which you can then redeem for flights to the Maldives or other travel expenses.

Firstly, it's worth noting that the Maldives has one main international airport, Velana International Airport (MLE), located on the island of Hulhulé. This is the primary entry point for most visitors to the Maldives, and most major airlines offer flights to MLE from various cities around the world.

If you're looking to save money on your flights to the Maldives, there are several strategies you can use:

Book in advance: As I mentioned earlier, booking your flights well in advance can often help you get a better deal. Many airlines offer early-bird discounts or special fares for bookings made several months ahead of time.

Look for deals and promotions: Keep an eye out for sales, promotions, and discount codes offered by airlines and travel companies. Signing up for newsletters and alerts can help you stay informed about the latest deals.

Be flexible with your travel dates: If you have some flexibility in your travel dates, you may be able to find cheaper flights. Traveling during the off-season, midweek, or on less popular travel days (like Tuesdays or Wednesdays) can sometimes save you money.

Consider alternative airports: Depending on where you're flying from, it may be cheaper to fly to a different airport and then take a connecting flight or ferry to the Maldives. For example, some visitors to the Maldives fly to nearby cities in Sri Lanka or India, and then take a short flight or boat ride to the Maldives.

Use travel rewards: As I mentioned earlier, using travel rewards points or miles can help offset the cost of your flights. Many airlines and credit card companies offer travel rewards programs that allow you to earn points or miles with each purchase, which you can then redeem for flights to the Maldives or other travel expenses.

By using these strategies, you may be able to save money on your flights to the Maldives, and make your dream vacation to this tropical paradise more affordable.

Overall, flights to the Maldives can be pricey, but with careful planning and a bit of research, you can find ways to save on your travel expenses and make your dream vacation to this tropical paradise a reality.

**Accommodation**
The Maldives is known for its luxurious resorts, which can cost anywhere from $300 to $3,000 per night, depending on the level of luxury and the season. Some resorts offer all-inclusive packages that include meals, drinks, and activities, which can help you save money. If you're looking for a more budget-friendly option, there are guesthouses and hotels available on local islands, which can cost anywhere from $50 to $200 per night.

**Food**
Food in the Maldives can be quite expensive, especially at resort restaurants. On average, expect to pay $30 to $50 per person for a meal at a resort restaurant, but prices can go up from there depending on the level of luxury. If you're staying at a guesthouse or hotel on a local island, you'll find more affordable options, with meals costing around $10 to $20 per person.

**Activities**
The Maldives is known for its beautiful beaches and stunning coral reefs, and there are plenty of activities to enjoy, such as snorkeling, scuba diving,

and surfing. Prices for activities can vary, but expect to pay around $50 to $100 per person for a snorkeling or diving excursion. Surfing lessons can cost anywhere from $50 to $150 per person.

**Transportation**
Transportation in the Maldives can be expensive, especially if you're traveling between islands. Seaplane transfers from Male International Airport to your resort can cost anywhere from $300 to $600 per person, depending on the distance. If you're staying on a local island, expect to pay around $5 to $20 per person for a ferry ride.

Overall, the cost of a trip to the Maldives can vary greatly depending on your travel style and the level of luxury you're looking for. If you're on a budget, consider staying on a local island and choosing more affordable activities and restaurants. However, if you're looking for a luxurious and indulgent vacation, expect to pay top dollar for the best resorts and amenities.

**Taxes and Fees**

When traveling to the Maldives, there are a few taxes and fees to be aware of. The first is the Maldives Tourism Goods and Services Tax (T-GST), which is a 12% tax on all goods and services purchased in the Maldives, including accommodation and food. There's also a Green Tax of $6 per person per night, which goes towards environmental protection and sustainability efforts in the Maldives.

**Currency**

The local currency in the Maldives is the Maldivian Rufiyaa (MVR), but US dollars are widely accepted at resorts and tourist areas. However, it's a good idea to have some local currency on hand for purchases at local markets and restaurants.

**Seasonality**

The cost of a trip to the Maldives can also vary depending on the time of year you plan to travel. The high season in the Maldives is from December to April, which is when the weather is dry and sunny. During this time, expect to pay higher prices for flights and accommodation. The low season is from May to November, which is when the weather is more unpredictable and there's a higher chance of rain. However, prices for flights and accommodation can be lower during this time.

**Tips**
While tipping is not expected in the Maldives, it's appreciated for exceptional service. At restaurants, a 10% service charge is often added to the bill, but you can still leave a small tip if you feel the service was exceptional. For activities, a small tip of $5 to $10 per person is a nice gesture for guides and instructors.

# Backpacking Maldives Recommended Budgets

Backpacking in the Maldives may not be as popular as staying in a luxurious resort, but it's still possible to enjoy this beautiful destination on a budget. Here are some recommended budgets for backpacking in the Maldives:

## 1. Budget Accommodation

While there are many luxurious resorts in the Maldives, there are also guesthouses and budget hotels available on local islands. These accommodations can cost anywhere from $50 to $200 per night, depending on the island and the level of comfort. Guesthouses typically offer basic amenities, such as air conditioning, Wi-Fi, and breakfast.

## 2. Food

Food in the Maldives can be expensive, especially at resort restaurants. If you're staying at a guesthouse or hotel on a local island, you'll find more affordable options, with meals costing around $10 to $20 per person. Local restaurants and cafes offer traditional Maldivian cuisine, which is a mix of Indian, Sri Lankan, and Arabic flavors.

### 3. Transportation

Transportation in the Maldives can be expensive, especially if you're traveling between islands. Seaplane transfers from Male International Airport to your island can cost anywhere from $300 to $600 per person, depending on the distance. If you're staying on a local island, expect to pay around $5 to $20 per person for a ferry ride.

### 4. Activities

The Maldives is known for its beautiful beaches and stunning coral reefs, which can be enjoyed on a budget. Snorkeling is a popular activity and can be done for free at some beaches or for a small fee if you rent snorkeling gear. There are also plenty of local tours and activities available, such as island hopping, fishing, and dolphin watching, which can cost around $20 to $50 per person.

### 5. Recommended Budgets

If you're backpacking in the Maldives, here are some recommended budgets:

Budget Backpacker: $50 to $80 per day. This budget includes staying in a guesthouse or budget hotel, eating at local restaurants, and enjoying free or low-cost activities.

**6. Mid-Range Backpacker $80 to $150 per day** This budget includes staying in a mid-range hotel, eating at a mix of local restaurants and resort restaurants, and enjoying a mix of free and paid activities.

**7. Luxury Backpacker $150 to $300 per day** This budget includes staying in a luxurious hotel or resort, eating at high-end restaurants, and enjoying a range of paid activities and excursions.

Overall, backpacking in the Maldives can be a more affordable way to experience this stunning destination. With a bit of planning and budgeting, it's possible to have a wonderful and memorable trip without breaking the bank.

## Maldives Money Saving Tips

If you're planning a trip to the Maldives, it's no secret that it can be an expensive destination. However, with some smart planning and budgeting, it's possible to save money while still enjoying everything the Maldives has to offer. Here are some money-saving tips for your Maldives trip:

**1. Travel during the low season:** The high season in the Maldives is from December to April, which is when prices for flights, accommodation, and activities are at their peak. Consider traveling during the low season from May to November, when prices can be up to 30% lower.

**2. Stay on a local island:** While the Maldives is known for its luxurious resorts, there are also guesthouses and budget hotels on local islands that offer more affordable accommodations. This is a great way to experience local culture and save money at the same time.

**3. Use public transportation:** If you're staying on a local island, use public transportation, such as ferries, to get around. This is a much more affordable option than hiring a private speedboat or seaplane transfer.

**4. Eat at local restaurants:** Dining at resort restaurants can be expensive, so consider eating at local restaurants or cafes instead. You'll find more affordable options and have the opportunity to try traditional Maldivian cuisine.

**5. Bring your own snorkeling gear:** Snorkeling is a popular activity in the Maldives, but renting gear from resorts or tour operators can be expensive. Bring your own snorkeling gear to save money and enjoy the underwater beauty of the Maldives.

**6. Book activities and excursions through local providers:** While resort excursions can be convenient, they can also be expensive. Look for local providers offering tours and activities, and compare prices before booking.

**7. Negotiate prices:** Don't be afraid to negotiate prices when shopping at local markets or booking transportation. Many vendors are open to bargaining and you can often get a better deal by asking for a lower price.

**8. Avoid alcoholic:** Alcohol is heavily taxed in the Maldives, and drinks at resorts and restaurants can be expensive. Consider skipping alcohol altogether or limiting your consumption to save money.

**9. Book in advance:** Booking flights and accommodations well in advance can help you save money. Many airlines and hotels offer early bird discounts, so start planning your trip early to take advantage of these deals.

**10. Look for package deals:** Many travel companies offer package deals for the Maldives that include flights, accommodation, and activities. These can be a great way to save money and get the most out of your trip.

**11. Use credit card points:** If you have a travel rewards credit card, consider using your points to pay for flights or accommodation. This can help you save money and get more value out of your credit card rewards.

**12. Limit souvenir shopping:** While it can be tempting to buy souvenirs to remember your trip, shopping in the Maldives can be expensive. Consider limiting your souvenir shopping or looking for more affordable options, such as locally-made crafts or snacks.

**13. Use free activities:** There are many free activities to enjoy in the Maldives, such as strolling along the beaches, watching sunsets, or exploring local villages. Take advantage of these free activities to save money and experience the local culture.

**14. Bring your own water bottle:** Buying bottled water in the Maldives can be expensive, so bring your own reusable water bottle and refill it from a water station or tap.

**15. Consider a shorter trip:** Instead of staying in the Maldives for a week or more, consider a shorter trip to save money. You can still enjoy the beautiful beaches and activities in a shorter amount of time, and it will be easier on your wallet.

By following these tips, you can save money while still enjoying all the beauty and excitement of the Maldives. With a bit of planning and budgeting, your Maldives trip can be affordable and memorable.

## How to Travel Around Maldives

With over 1,000 islands scattered throughout the archipelago, getting around the Maldives can seem daunting. However, with a little planning and preparation, navigating the Maldives can be a breeze. Here are some tips on how to travel around the Maldives:

**By seaplane:**
One of the most popular ways to get around the Maldives is by seaplane. Many resorts and hotels have their own seaplanes that can transport guests from the main international airport to their island resort. The views from the seaplane are stunning, and it's an experience in itself.

**By speedboat:**
Another way to get around the Maldives is by speedboat. Many resorts offer speedboat transfers to and from the airport or other islands. Speedboats are a great option for shorter distances and can get you to your destination quickly.

**By ferry:**
If you're traveling on a budget, taking a ferry is an option. Public ferries connect some of the islands in the Maldives, and it's a great way to see local life and experience the Maldives from a different perspective. However, be prepared for longer travel times and limited schedules.

**By private yacht:**
For a luxurious experience, consider renting a private yacht to explore the Maldives. You can explore multiple islands and atolls at your own pace and enjoy the privacy and luxury that comes with traveling by yacht.

**By bicycle or foot:**
Once you're on an island, one of the best ways to get around is by bicycle or foot. Many resorts provide bicycles for guests, and it's a fun and eco-friendly way to explore the island. Walking is also a great way to get exercise and take in the beauty of the Maldives.

In conclusion, getting around the Maldives can be an adventure in itself, and there are many ways to explore this beautiful country. Whether you're traveling by seaplane, speedboat, ferry, private yacht, bicycle, or foot, be prepared for stunning views and unforgettable experiences.

## How to be Safe in Maldives

Maldives is a beautiful country with pristine beaches and crystal-clear waters. However, like any tourist destination, safety should be a top priority for visitors. Here are some tips on how to be safe in Maldives:

**1. Be mindful of the ocean:** The Maldives is known for its stunning coral reefs, but the ocean can be dangerous, especially during monsoon season. Always check with locals or your hotel staff before going into the water, and never swim alone. Also, be aware of strong currents and rip tides.

**2. Respect the local culture:** Maldives is an Islamic country, so it's important to respect local customs and dress modestly when outside of your resort. Alcohol is also prohibited outside of resorts and private homes, so be mindful of this if you plan on drinking.

**3. Watch out for scams:** Tourists are sometimes targeted by scammers, so be wary of people who approach you offering tours or other services.

Always use a reputable tour company, and don't give money or personal information to strangers.

**4. Protect yourself from the sun:** The Maldives is a tropical country, so the sun can be intense. Wear sunscreen, a hat, and sunglasses to protect yourself from sunburn and heatstroke. Drink plenty of water to stay hydrated.

**5. Be careful when traveling:** If you're traveling between islands, be sure to use a reputable ferry or speedboat service. Avoid traveling at night, and always wear a lifejacket.

**6. Keep your belongings safe:** Petty theft can occur in tourist areas, so keep your valuables in a safe place, such as a hotel safe. Don't leave your belongings unattended on the beach or in public areas.

**7. Get travel insurance:** Finally, make sure you have comprehensive travel insurance that covers medical emergencies, evacuation, and theft. It's better to be safe than sorry.

**8. Know the emergency numbers:** In case of an emergency, you should know the emergency phone numbers for Maldives. The police emergency number is 119, and the ambulance service can be reached at 102. Keep these numbers saved in your phone, and know the location of the nearest hospital or medical facility.

**9. Be careful with alcohol:** If you plan on drinking alcohol while in the Maldives, be mindful of your alcohol consumption, as excessive drinking can impair your judgment and increase your risk of accidents or becoming a victim of crime. Also, remember that alcohol is prohibited outside of resorts and private homes, so always drink responsibly and within the designated areas.

**10. Stay informed about local news:** Stay up to date with the latest news and events in Maldives, especially if you plan on traveling to different islands or participating in outdoor activities. In the event of civil unrest, natural disasters, or other emergencies, stay informed and follow the advice of local authorities.

**11. Use caution when engaging in water sports:** Maldives is a popular destination for water sports like snorkeling, scuba diving, and surfing. However, it's important to use caution and only participate in these activities with a reputable company or guide. Always wear proper safety equipment, and follow the instructions of your guide.

**12. Be mindful of wildlife:** Maldives is home to a variety of wildlife, including sharks, stingrays, and jellyfish. While these creatures are generally harmless, it's important to be aware of their presence and take precautions to avoid any potential risks. Don't touch or feed wildlife, and always listen to the advice of your guide.

By following these tips, you can have a safe and enjoyable trip to the Maldives. Remember to always be vigilant, use common sense, and respect the local culture.

Maldives is generally considered a safe country for tourists and locals alike. However, like any other destination, there is always a risk of crime and other safety concerns.

If you are in Maldives and feel unsafe, there are a few things you can expect:

**Contact the authorities:** If you feel threatened or unsafe, immediately contact the local authorities, such as the police. They can provide assistance and guidance on how to stay safe.

**Use common sense:** Just like in any other country, it's important to use common sense and be aware of your surroundings. Avoid going to isolated or poorly lit areas, especially at night. Be cautious of strangers and don't leave your belongings unattended.

**Stay in a safe accommodation:** Make sure to choose a reputable and safe accommodation. Check the reviews of the hotel or resort you plan to stay at, and opt for one that has good security measures in place.

**Be cautious of scams:** Be wary of scams, such as fake tour operators, and only use reputable tour companies that have good reviews.

**Seek medical attention if needed:** If you are injured or sick, seek medical attention immediately. There are several hospitals and clinics in Maldives that can provide medical assistance.

Overall, it's important to exercise caution and common sense when traveling to any destination, including Maldives. By being aware of your surroundings and taking necessary precautions, you can help ensure a safe and enjoyable trip.

# The Maldives Tourist Visa

The Maldives is a beautiful tropical paradise located in the Indian Ocean, known for its pristine beaches, crystal clear waters, and vibrant marine life. As a popular tourist destination, visitors from all over the world flock to the Maldives to enjoy its beauty and experience its unique culture.

If you are planning to visit the Maldives for tourism purposes, you will need to obtain a tourist visa before your trip. In this article, we will cover all the essential details you need to know about the Maldives tourist visa.

## Who needs a Maldives tourist visa?

All foreign visitors who wish to enter the Maldives for tourism purposes must obtain a tourist visa, except for citizens of the following countries:

Maldives
Seychelles
Mauritius
Singapore
These countries have a visa-free agreement with the Maldives, and their citizens can enter the country without a visa for up to 30 days.

## How to apply for a Maldives tourist visa?

To apply for a Maldives tourist visa, you need to contact the Maldives Embassy or Consulate in your country. You can find the contact details and visa requirements on the embassy's website.

The documents required for a Maldives tourist visa application include:

A valid passport with at least 6 months validity remaining
Completed visa application form
Passport size photograph
Confirmed return air ticket
Proof of accommodation booking in the Maldives
Proof of sufficient funds for your stay in the Maldives
The visa application fee varies depending on your nationality, and it is non-refundable even if your visa application is rejected.

## How long is the Maldives tourist visa valid for?

The Maldives tourist visa is typically valid for 30 days from the date of entry into the country. If you wish to stay for longer than 30 days, you can apply for an extension from the Maldives Immigration Department.

## Can I extend my Maldives tourist visa?

Yes, it is possible to extend your Maldives tourist visa for up to 90 days. To apply for an extension, you need to visit the Maldives Immigration Department in Malé, the capital city, at least two weeks before your visa expires. You will need to provide the following documents:

Passport and visa copy
Completed visa extension application form
Confirmed return air ticket
Proof of accommodation booking in the Maldives
Proof of sufficient funds for your extended stay in the Maldives

It is important to note that the Maldives Immigration Department has the final say on whether to approve or reject your visa extension application.

**Conclusion**

Obtaining a Maldives tourist visa is a straightforward process, and it is a necessary requirement for all foreign visitors who wish to visit the Maldives for tourism purposes. Make sure to apply for your visa well in advance of your trip, and ensure that you have all the required documents and sufficient funds to support your stay in the Maldives. With your visa in hand, you can look forward to an unforgettable holiday in this beautiful island nation.

Certainly! In addition to the basic information provided earlier, here are some more details you may find helpful if you are planning to apply for a Maldives tourist visa:

**Visa on Arrival**: If you are a citizen of a country that requires a tourist visa, you may be eligible for a visa on arrival if you have a valid passport and proof of sufficient funds for your stay in the Maldives. However, this option is only available for stays of up to 30 days.

**Visa Processing Time**: The processing time for a Maldives tourist visa varies depending on the embassy or consulate and your nationality. In general, it takes between 3 to 7 working days for a visa application to be processed.

**Visa Fees:** The visa fee for a Maldives tourist visa varies depending on your nationality. The fee is usually payable in your local currency, and it is non-refundable even if your visa application is rejected.

**Travel Insurance**: It is recommended that you have travel insurance that covers medical emergencies and accidents during your stay in the Maldives. Some embassies and consulates may require proof of travel insurance as part of the visa application process.

**Passport Requirements**: Your passport must be valid for at least 6 months from the date of entry into the Maldives. It should also have at least two blank pages for visa stamps.

**Restricted Items:** The Maldives has strict rules on importing and exporting certain items, such as drugs, weapons, and pornography. Make sure you are familiar with these rules before you travel to avoid any legal issues.

**COVID-19 Requirements**: Due to the ongoing COVID-19 pandemic, visitors to the Maldives may be required to follow specific entry requirements, such as providing proof of vaccination, a negative COVID-19 test result, or undergoing quarantine upon arrival. Make sure to check the latest travel guidelines before your trip.

We hope this additional information helps you plan your trip to the Maldives and apply for your tourist visa with confidence. Enjoy your stay in this beautiful island paradise!

# 10 Days in Maldives

If you're planning to visit the Maldives, 10 days is a good amount of time to spend in this island paradise. Here is a sample itinerary for a 10-day trip to the Maldives:

**Day 1: Maafushi Island Tour**

Day 1 of your Maafushi Island Tour is sure to be an exciting start to your vacation in the Maldives. Maafushi Island is located in the South Male Atoll and is one of the most popular local islands to visit in the Maldives.

You can start your day with a delicious breakfast at your hotel or guesthouse on Maafushi Island. Then, head out to explore the island's beautiful beaches, turquoise waters, and stunning coral reefs. Maafushi Island has plenty of options for snorkeling, diving, and other water sports activities.

One of the highlights of Maafushi Island is the Bikini Beach, which is an exclusive beach designated for tourists. Here, you can relax on the soft white sands, soak up the sun, and swim in the crystal-clear waters of the Indian Ocean. The beach is also an ideal spot for snorkeling, and you can rent snorkeling gear and explore the underwater world of the Maldives.

In the afternoon, take a stroll through the bustling streets of Maafushi Island and soak up the local culture. You can visit the local souvenir shops, try out some delicious Maldivian cuisine at the island's restaurants, and even catch a glimpse of the local way of life by visiting the local mosque and fishing harbor.

As the sun sets, head back to Bikini Beach and watch the spectacular sunset over the ocean. You can relax on the beach or take a sunset cruise to see the beauty of the island from the water.

Finally, end your day with a delicious dinner at one of the island's many restaurants, followed by a relaxing walk on the beach under the starry night sky.

Overall, Day 1 of your Maafushi Island Tour is a perfect introduction to the beauty and charm of the Maldives. With so much to see and do on Maafushi Island, you're sure to have an unforgettable experience.

## Where to stay in Maafushi Island Tour

Here are some of the best places to stay on Maafushi Island:

Arena Beach Hotel - This hotel is located on the beachfront, and it offers comfortable rooms with modern amenities such as air conditioning, flat-screen TVs, and free Wi-Fi. The hotel also has a restaurant, a rooftop terrace, and a spa.

Crystal Sands Beach Hotel - This beachfront hotel features spacious rooms with air conditioning, flat-screen TVs, and minibars. The hotel also has a restaurant, a bar, and a spa.

Kaani Grand Seaview - This hotel is located on the beachfront, and it offers spacious rooms with air conditioning, flat-screen TVs, and minibars. The hotel also has a rooftop terrace, a restaurant, and a spa.

Holiday Lodge - This guesthouse is located near the beach, and it offers affordable rooms with air conditioning, flat-screen TVs, and free Wi-Fi. The guesthouse also has a restaurant, a bar, and a garden.

Serene Sky Guest House - This guest house is located near the beach, and it offers cozy rooms with air conditioning, flat-screen TVs, and free Wi-Fi. The guesthouse also has a rooftop terrace, a restaurant, and a garden.

Summer Villa Guest House - This guest house is located near the beach, and it offers comfortable rooms with air conditioning, flat-screen TVs, and free Wi-Fi. The guesthouse also has a restaurant, a bar, and a garden.

No matter where you choose to stay on Maafushi Island, you're sure to have a comfortable and enjoyable vacation. Just make sure to book your accommodation in advance, especially during peak season, as the island can get quite busy with tourists.

**Day 2: Scuba Diving on Maafushi**

Day 2 of your Maafushi Island Tour is all about exploring the underwater world of the Maldives. Maafushi Island is known for its stunning coral reefs, abundant marine life, and clear turquoise waters, making it a perfect destination for scuba diving.

Start your day with an early breakfast and then head out to the dive center to begin your scuba diving adventure. There are several dive centers on the island that offer a range of courses, from beginner to advanced, so you can choose the one that best suits your skill level.

Once you're ready, you'll be taken on a boat ride to one of the nearby dive sites. The dive sites around Maafushi Island are home to a variety of marine life, including reef sharks, turtles, rays, and colorful fish. You'll be able to see the beauty of the coral reefs up close and swim among the different species of marine life.

If you're a beginner, don't worry, the dive center will provide you with all the necessary equipment and training. You'll be accompanied by an experienced dive instructor who will guide you through the dive and ensure your safety throughout the experience.

After your dive, you can relax on the beach, enjoy a refreshing drink or snack, and relive your underwater adventure.

In the afternoon, you can explore more of the island's attractions, such as the Maafushi Prison or the Maafushi Mosque. You can also visit the local souvenir shops and pick up some unique Maldivian handicrafts to take home as a souvenir.

Finally, end your day with a delicious dinner at one of the island's many restaurants, where you can try some authentic Maldivian cuisine, including fresh seafood and traditional curries.

Overall, Day 2 of your Maafushi Island Tour is an exciting and adventurous day that will give you a unique and unforgettable experience of the Maldives' underwater world.

## Where to stay Maafushi for scuba diving

Here are some options for where to stay in Maafushi for scuba diving:

Maafushi Inn - This cozy inn is located just a short walk from the beach and offers comfortable rooms at an affordable price. The inn also has its own dive center, making it a convenient choice for scuba diving enthusiasts.

Kaani Beach Hotel - This modern hotel is situated right on the beach and has its own dive center. The hotel offers spacious and well-equipped rooms, and its central location makes it easy to access all the best dive sites in Maafushi.

Arena Lodge Maldives - This budget-friendly lodge is a great choice for those looking for basic accommodation at an affordable price. The lodge is located near the beach and has its own dive center, making it a convenient choice for scuba diving enthusiasts.

Arena Beach Hotel - This beachfront hotel is ideal for those looking for a bit more luxury. The hotel offers spacious rooms and suites, an infinity pool, and its own dive center. It's located just a short walk from the beach and all the best dive sites in Maafushi.

Adaaran Select Hudhuranfushi - For those seeking a more upscale experience, this resort is an excellent choice. The resort offers luxurious overwater villas, multiple restaurants, and its own dive center. It's located on a private island just a short boat ride away from Maafushi.

## Day 3: Experience Maafushi's water sports

Day 3 on Maafushi island in the Maldives is a perfect time to experience the thrilling water sports that the island has to offer. With its crystal clear waters and vibrant marine life, Maafushi is an ideal destination for adrenaline junkies looking to try their hand at a variety of water sports. Here are some of the best water sports to try on Day 3:

Jet Skiing - Jet skiing is a thrilling way to explore the beautiful coastline of Maafushi. You can rent a jet ski and hit the waves solo, or take a guided tour and discover hidden coves and stunning scenery.

Snorkeling - Maafushi's waters are home to a diverse array of marine life, making it an ideal destination for snorkeling. You can rent snorkeling gear and explore the coral reefs and underwater caves on your own, or take a guided tour to get the most out of your experience.

Scuba Diving - Scuba diving is one of the best ways to experience the incredible underwater world around Maafushi. Whether you're a beginner or an experienced diver, there are dive sites to suit all levels. You can take a guided tour and explore the colorful coral reefs and fascinating sea creatures, or even try your hand at night diving for a unique experience.

Parasailing - Parasailing is a great way to get a bird's eye view of Maafushi's stunning coastline. You can take a solo ride or go with a partner, and soar above the turquoise waters while taking in the breathtaking views.

Kayaking - Kayaking is a fun and relaxing way to explore Maafushi's beautiful lagoons and mangrove forests. You can rent a kayak and paddle around the island's calm waters at your own pace, taking in the natural beauty of the island.

**Where to stay in Maafushi's water sports**

Arena Lodge Maldives - This budget-friendly lodge is located just a short walk from the beach and offers easy access to Maafushi's water sports. The lodge has its own dive center and water sports facilities, making it a convenient choice for those looking to stay active on the water.

Crystal Sands Beach Hotel - This beachfront hotel offers stunning views of the turquoise waters surrounding Maafushi. The hotel has its own water sports center and offers a variety of activities, including jet skiing, snorkeling, and kayaking.

Kaani Beach Hotel - This modern hotel is located right on the beach and has its own water sports center. The hotel offers spacious and well-equipped rooms, making it a comfortable choice for those looking to relax after a day on the water.

Ocean Vista Guesthouse - This guesthouse is situated just a short walk from the beach and offers easy access to Maafushi's water sports. The guesthouse has its own water sports center and offers a range of activities, including scuba diving, snorkeling, and parasailing.

Adaaran Prestige Ocean Villas - For those seeking a more luxurious experience, this resort is an excellent choice. The resort is located on a private island just a short boat ride away from Maafushi and offers overwater villas with stunning views of the ocean. The resort has its own water sports center and offers a variety of activities, including jet skiing, snorkeling, and kayaking.

## Day 4: A visit to Himmafushi Island

On Day 4 of your trip to Maafushi, it's time to explore the nearby island of Himmafushi. Located just a short boat ride away, Himmafushi is a charming island with a rich cultural heritage and stunning natural beauty. Here are some of the things to see and do on your visit to Himmafushi:

Visit the local mosque - Himmafushi is home to one of the oldest mosques in the Maldives, the Kuda Miskiy Mosque. This beautiful mosque is made entirely of coral stone and offers a glimpse into the island's rich history and culture.

Take a tour of the island - Himmafushi is a small island that's easy to explore on foot. Take a leisurely stroll through the island's narrow streets and see the traditional houses, shops, and cafes. You can also hire a local guide to show you around and share insights about the island's history and culture.

Learn about traditional handicrafts - Himmafushi is known for its traditional handicrafts, including intricate lacquer work and beautiful woven mats. You can visit local workshops and see artisans at work, or even try your hand at making your own handicrafts.

Relax on the beach - Himmafushi has several beautiful beaches where you can relax and soak up the sun. North Beach is a popular spot with soft white sand and clear blue waters, perfect for swimming and sunbathing.

Go fishing - Himmafushi is famous for its traditional fishing industry, and you can experience it firsthand by going on a fishing trip with a local fisherman. You can catch your own fish and even learn how to prepare it the traditional way.

Overall, a visit to Himmafushi is a great way to experience the authentic culture and natural beauty of the Maldives. Don't forget to bring your camera to capture the stunning scenery and unique experiences on this charming island.

## Where to stay in Himmafushi Island

Himmafushi Island Guesthouse - This guesthouse is located on the island itself and offers comfortable rooms with modern amenities. The guesthouse also has a restaurant and can arrange activities such as snorkeling and fishing.

Ripple Beach Inn - This beachfront guesthouse is located on a nearby island and offers easy access to Himmafushi Island. The inn offers spacious rooms with stunning ocean views and a range of facilities, including a restaurant, spa, and water sports activities.

Dhonveli View - This guesthouse is also located on a nearby island and offers affordable rooms with modern amenities. The guesthouse has a rooftop terrace with beautiful views and offers activities such as snorkeling, fishing, and island hopping tours.

Four Seasons Resort Maldives at Kuda Huraa - For a more luxurious experience, this resort is located on a private island near Himmafushi and offers overwater villas with stunning ocean views. The resort has its own private beach, a spa, and a range of water sports activities.

Paradise Island Resort & Spa - This all-inclusive resort is located on a nearby island and offers a range of accommodation options, including beachfront villas and overwater bungalows. The resort has its own private beach, a spa, and a range of activities, including snorkeling, diving, and fishing.

**Day 5: Fulidhoo Island Tour**

On Day 5 of your trip to Maafushi, it's time to visit the picturesque Fulidhoo Island. This stunning island is located in the Vaavu Atoll and is famous for its crystal-clear waters, pristine beaches, and colorful coral reefs. Here are some of the things to see and do on your visit to Fulidhoo Island:

Snorkeling and diving - Fulidhoo Island is home to some of the best snorkeling and diving spots in the Maldives. The island's shallow lagoons are teeming with marine life, including colorful fish, sea turtles, and even reef sharks. You can rent snorkeling and diving equipment on the island or book a guided tour with a local operator.

Explore the island's beaches - Fulidhoo Island is home to several beautiful beaches, including the main beach on the eastern side of the island. The beach has soft white sand and crystal-clear waters, perfect for swimming, sunbathing, and beach games.

Visit the local village - Fulidhoo Island has a small local village where you can experience the local Maldivian culture and way of life. You can visit the island's mosque, see traditional houses, and even try some local cuisine at one of the island's cafes or restaurants.

Take a sunset cruise - One of the best ways to experience the beauty of Fulidhoo Island is to take a sunset cruise around the island. You can watch the sun dip below the horizon while sipping on a refreshing drink and enjoying the cool ocean breeze.

Try some water sports - Fulidhoo Island offers a range of water sports activities, including kayaking, stand-up paddleboarding, and windsurfing. You can rent equipment on the island or book a guided tour with a local operator.

**Where to stay in Fulidhoo Island**

Thundi Guest House - This guest house is located on the eastern side of the island, just a few steps away from the beach. The guest house offers comfortable rooms with modern amenities, including air conditioning, free Wi-Fi, and private bathrooms. The guest house also has a restaurant and can arrange activities such as snorkeling, diving, and fishing.

Raakani Lodge - This guest house is located on the western side of the island, close to the island's main jetty. The guest house offers cozy rooms with simple decor and basic amenities, including air conditioning and private bathrooms. The guest house also has a restaurant and can arrange activities such as snorkeling and diving.

Fulidhoo Dive & Water Sports - If you're looking for a more active holiday, this guest house is located on the eastern side of the island and offers a range of water sports activities, including diving, snorkeling, and windsurfing. The guest house offers comfortable rooms with air conditioning and private bathrooms, as well as a restaurant and a dive center.

Thundi Villa - This beachfront guest house is located on the eastern side of the island and offers spacious rooms with stunning ocean views. The guest house also has a restaurant and can arrange activities such as snorkeling, diving, and fishing.

Thundi Beach Resort - This luxury resort is located on a nearby private island and offers overwater villas with stunning ocean views. The resort has its own private beach, a spa, and a range of water sports activities, including snorkeling, diving, and fishing.

## Day 6: Extra fun on Fulidhoo Island

Fulidhoo Island offers plenty of opportunities for fun and adventure beyond its beautiful beaches and crystal-clear waters. Here are some extra activities to consider for an unforgettable experience on the island:

Island hopping - Fulidhoo Island is located in the Vaavu Atoll, which is home to several other islands worth exploring. You can arrange a guided tour with a local operator or rent a boat to explore nearby islands like Keyodhoo, Alimathaa, and Thinadhoo.

Night fishing - Experience the traditional Maldivian way of fishing by going on a night fishing trip. You'll board a local fishing boat and try your hand at catching snapper, grouper, and other local fish species. The tour operator will provide all the necessary equipment, and you can even have your catch prepared for dinner back at your accommodation.

Beach games - The beaches on Fulidhoo Island are perfect for playing beach volleyball, soccer, or frisbee. Bring your own gear or rent equipment from your accommodation and enjoy a fun-filled day on the beach with family or friends.

Local cuisine - Fulidhoo Island has several cafes and restaurants where you can sample traditional Maldivian cuisine. Don't miss out on trying local favorites like mas huni (tuna and coconut salad), garudhiya (fish soup), and roshi (flatbread).

Stargazing - With little light pollution on the island, Fulidhoo is a great place to observe the night sky. Lay on the beach or your accommodation's rooftop and enjoy the stunning starry night sky.

Surfing - If you're an experienced surfer, you can take a boat ride to nearby surf breaks such as Kandooma Right or Riptides. You can rent surfboards on the island or bring your own.

## Day 7: Rasdhoo Island Tour

Rasdhoo is a small island with a population of around 1,500 people and is a popular destination for tourists who come to experience the Maldives' famous turquoise waters, white sandy beaches, and vibrant marine life.

The island is about 60 kilometers west of the capital city, Male, and is accessible via a speedboat ride or a seaplane. Upon arrival, you'll be greeted by the friendly locals who will show you around and make sure you have a memorable stay.

One of the highlights of visiting Rasdhoo Island is exploring its surrounding waters. The island is surrounded by a beautiful coral reef that is teeming with diverse marine life. Snorkeling and diving are popular activities, and you can see everything from schools of colorful fish to sea turtles, stingrays, and even reef sharks.

For those who prefer to stay on land, Rasdhoo Island also has plenty to offer. You can take a stroll along the island's pristine beaches, bask in the sun, and relax under the shade of swaying palm trees. You can also take a bike tour around the island to see the local way of life and visit the island's cultural landmarks, such as the local mosque and the old cemetery.

In addition, Rasdhoo Island is also home to several restaurants and cafes serving up traditional Maldivian cuisine, such as spicy fish curries, coconut-based dishes, and fresh seafood. You can also find international cuisine options such as Italian, Chinese and Western dishes.

Finally, don't forget to catch the island's stunning sunsets that paint the sky with hues of orange, pink, and purple. The sky, combined with the gentle breeze, create an ambiance of serenity and peace.

In conclusion, Rasdhoo Island is a must-visit destination for anyone traveling to the Maldives. With its incredible marine life, beautiful beaches, and warm hospitality, it is a paradise that will leave you in awe and wanting more.

**Where to stay in Rasdhoo Island**

Here are some of the popular options:

Guesthouses: Guesthouses are a popular choice for budget-conscious travelers who prefer a more local experience. They offer clean and comfortable rooms with basic amenities such as air conditioning, hot water, and Wi-Fi. Some popular guesthouses on Rasdhoo Island include Rasdhoo Island Inn, Island Cottage, and Rasdhoo View Inn.

Boutique hotels: For those looking for a more luxurious experience, boutique hotels on Rasdhoo Island offer stylish accommodations with high-end amenities such as private pools, spa services, and gourmet dining. Some of the top boutique hotels on Rasdhoo Island include Kuramathi Maldives, Nika Island Resort & Spa, and Athiri Inn.

Hostels: For solo travelers or backpackers, hostels are a great option for budget accommodation. Rasdhoo Island has a few hostels that offer dormitory-style rooms with shared bathrooms and communal areas for socializing. Some of the popular hostels on the island include Friends Residence, Rashdoo Retreat, and Residence Rasko.

## Day 8: Manta Ray Diving on Rasdhoo Island

If you're a fan of scuba diving, then a Manta Ray diving experience on Rasdhoo Island should definitely be on your bucket list. Manta Ray diving is a unique and unforgettable experience that will allow you to witness these gentle giants up close in their natural habitat.

Manta Rays are one of the largest species of ray and can grow up to 7 meters in width. They are found in the waters around the Maldives and are known for their graceful movements and impressive acrobatics. Manta Rays feed on plankton and are harmless to humans, making them an ideal species to observe up close.

To go Manta Ray diving on Rasdhoo Island, you'll need to book a tour with a reputable diving center. Most diving centers offer guided tours that include a boat ride to the diving site, all necessary diving equipment, and an experienced guide who will help you spot the Manta Rays.

The best time to go Manta Ray diving on Rasdhoo Island is between the months of November to April when the water is calm, and the visibility is good.

During this time, Manta Rays can be seen in large numbers as they gather in the area to feed.

As you descend into the water, you'll be amazed by the clarity of the water and the vibrant colors of the coral reef. Soon after, you'll spot the Manta Rays as they gracefully glide through the water, often performing somersaults and flips. The experience is truly mesmerizing, and you'll be in awe of the beauty of these creatures.

Manta Ray diving on Rasdhoo Island is a must-do activity for any diving enthusiast or nature lover visiting the Maldives. It's an unforgettable experience that will leave you with memories to cherish for a lifetime.

## Where to stay in Manta Ray Diving on Rasdhoo Island

Guesthouses: Guesthouses are a popular choice for budget-conscious travelers who prefer a more local experience. They offer clean and comfortable rooms with basic amenities such as air conditioning, hot water, and Wi-Fi. Some popular guesthouses on Rasdhoo Island include Rasdhoo Island Inn, Island Cottage, and Rasdhoo View Inn.

Diving resorts: For diving enthusiasts, there are several diving resorts on Rasdhoo Island that offer diving packages and equipment rental services. These resorts are often located close to diving sites, making it easy to access the waters. Some popular diving resorts on Rasdhoo Island include Rasdhoo Dive Lodge, Ocean Beach Inn, and Island Divers Inn.

Boutique hotels: For those looking for a more luxurious experience, boutique hotels on Rasdhoo Island offer stylish accommodations with high-end amenities such as private pools, spa services, and gourmet dining. Some of the top boutique hotels on Rasdhoo Island include Kuramathi Maldives, Nika Island Resort & Spa, and Athiri Inn.

**Day 9: Thoddo Island Tour**

On Day 9 of your travels, you decide to take a tour of Thoddo Island, located off the coast of the Maldives. Thoddo Island is known for its stunning beaches, crystal clear waters, and vibrant marine life.

You start your tour by taking a speedboat from Male, the capital city of the Maldives, to Thoddo Island. The boat ride is exhilarating, with the wind in your hair and the sun on your face. As you approach the island, you can see the white sand beaches and turquoise waters that make Thoddo Island so famous.

Once you arrive at the island, you are greeted by your tour guide, who takes you on a walking tour of the island. You learn about the history and culture of the Maldives, as well as the unique ecosystem that exists on Thoddo Island.

One of the highlights of the tour is a visit to the island's coral reef. You put on your snorkeling gear and jump into the water, where you are immediately surrounded by colorful fish, sea turtles, and even a few sharks! The coral reef is breathtaking, with vibrant colors and intricate patterns that seem to go on forever.

After your snorkeling adventure, you head back to the beach for a delicious lunch of grilled fish, fresh fruit, and coconut water. You take some time to relax on the beach, soaking up the sun and enjoying the peaceful surroundings.

In the afternoon, you take a boat tour around the island, where you can see more of the stunning coastline and spot dolphins jumping in the waves. You also visit a local fishing village, where you learn about the traditional way of life for the Maldivian people.

As the sun begins to set, you head back to Male, feeling grateful for the amazing experience you had on Thoddo Island. The island's natural beauty and unique culture have left a lasting impression, and you know that this will be a trip you will never forget.

**Where to stay in Thoddo Island**

Como Maalifushi: This is a luxurious resort that offers overwater villas and beach suites with stunning views of the Indian Ocean. The resort features a spa, fitness center, multiple dining options, and various water sports activities.

Six Senses Laamu: This is another high-end resort that offers eco-friendly villas over the water or on the beach. The resort has several restaurants, a spa, a gym, and a dive center.

Rahaa Resort: This is a mid-range resort that offers beach villas with private pools and direct access to the beach. The resort has a restaurant, a spa, and a dive center.

Mathiveri Inn: This is a budget-friendly option that offers basic rooms with air conditioning and private bathrooms. The inn has a restaurant and offers various excursions, including snorkeling and fishing.

Local guesthouses: Thoddo Island also has several local guesthouses that offer affordable accommodation and a chance to experience the local Maldivian culture. These guesthouses are typically smaller and offer basic amenities.

## Day 10: Discover more of Thoddo

On Day 10 of your trip to Thoddo Island, there are many exciting things to discover and explore. Here are some ideas to help you make the most of your day:

Snorkeling and diving: Thoddo Island is known for its crystal-clear waters and vibrant marine life, making it a perfect destination for snorkeling and diving. There are several dive sites around the island, where you can see colorful corals, reef sharks, turtles, and various fish species.

Island hopping: Thoddo Island is surrounded by several other small islands that are worth visiting. You can take a speedboat or a traditional Maldivian boat known as a dhoni and explore nearby islands like Felivaru and Maavelavaru. You can enjoy the stunning beaches, take a stroll around the islands, and even have a picnic.

Fishing: Fishing is a popular activity in Thoddo Island, and there are various types of fishing you can try, including traditional hand line fishing, night fishing, and big game fishing. You can rent a fishing boat or join a fishing tour and try your luck at catching fish like tuna, barracuda, and grouper.

Visit Thoddo Island's local village: Thoddo Island has a small local village where you can experience the local Maldivian culture and way of life. You can walk around the village, visit the local mosque, and even try local cuisine at one of the village's cafes.

Relax on the beach: After a few days of exploring and adventure, take some time to relax and soak up the sun on Thoddo Island's stunning beaches. You can also enjoy water sports activities like kayaking, paddleboarding, and windsurfing.

In conclusion, Day 10 on Thoddo Island can be filled with adventure, culture, and relaxation, and there's something for everyone to enjoy. So, get out there and discover more of Thoddo Island!

There is no need for a busy day on the last day in the Maldives. Enjoy every last second by visiting the beach, going snorkeling or taking plenty of pictures. Go get a cool coconut drink from a neighborhood seller after every sunset. Also, unwind along the shore on a swing or a chair.

# Maldives Culture; facts, customs and traditions

The Maldives culture is influenced by various factors, including its Islamic heritage, Indian, Sri Lankan, and Arab influences. Here are some interesting facts, customs, and traditions that characterize the Maldives culture.

**Language**: The official language of Maldives is Dhivehi, a language that has its roots in Sanskrit, with strong influences from Arabic and Hindi.

**Religion**: Islam is the official religion of Maldives, and its influence is evident in the daily life of the people. Friday is the weekly holiday, and the call to prayer can be heard throughout the day.

**Clothing**: The traditional dress for men is the sarong-like garment called a Mundu, which is worn with a shirt or a T-shirt. Women wear a dress called a Libaas, which covers the body from the shoulders to the ankles.

**Music and Dance**: The traditional music of Maldives is called boduberu, which is performed using drums, clapping, and singing. The dance forms of Maldives are called Dhandi Jehun and Bandiya Jehun.

**Food**: Maldivian cuisine is a blend of Indian, Sri Lankan, and Arabic influences. The staple food is rice and fish, and the most popular dish is called Mas Riha, a spicy fish curry.

**Traditional Sports**: The Maldives has several traditional sports, including a form of wrestling called Famaa, a game of skill and agility called Don Hiyala, and a form of martial arts called Ganda.

**Art and Craft**: Maldivian art and craft are known for intricate designs and bright colors. Traditional crafts include lacquer work, mat weaving, and traditional boat building.

**Festivals**: The Maldives celebrates several festivals throughout the year, including the Islamic festivals of Eid al-Fitr and Eid al-Adha, the National Day, and the Fishermen's Day.

**Hospitality**: The Maldives culture is known for its hospitality, and visitors are often welcomed with open arms. It is customary to remove shoes before entering someone's home, and it is considered polite to bring a small gift for the host.

**Environmental Conservation**: The Maldives is committed to environmental conservation, and several initiatives have been implemented to protect the country's natural resources, including the coral reefs and marine life.

**Hulhangu**: Hulhangu is a traditional Maldivian wedding ceremony, which involves several customs and rituals. It includes the groom's party arriving at the bride's home, exchanging gifts, and performing the ceremonial tying of the knot. The celebrations can last for several days.

**Islamic Heritage**: Islam was introduced to the Maldives in the 12th century, and since then, it has played a significant role in shaping the country's culture and traditions. The Maldives is a Sunni Muslim country, and Islamic values influence daily life, from dress codes to social interactions.

**Traditional Medicine**: Maldivians have been using traditional medicine to treat various ailments for centuries. Herbal remedies, massage therapy, and acupuncture are popular forms of traditional medicine.

**Dhoni**: Dhoni is a traditional Maldivian boat that has been used for fishing and transportation for centuries. These boats are made of wood and are still used by many Maldivian fishermen today.

**Maldivian Language**: Dhivehi, the official language of Maldives, has its unique script known as Thaana. Thaana script is written from right to left, and it has 24 letters.

**Conservation of Marine Life**: The Maldives is home to a diverse range of marine life, including coral reefs, sea turtles, and whale sharks. The government has implemented several conservation initiatives, including marine protected areas, to protect the country's marine biodiversity.

**Bodu Beru**: Bodu Beru is a popular traditional Maldivian music form that is performed using drums, clapping, and singing. The music is often accompanied by a dance performance, and the performances can last for several hours.

**Cultural Shows**: Several resorts and guesthouses in the Maldives offer cultural shows that showcase traditional music, dance, and costumes. These shows are a great way to experience the local culture and traditions.

**Maldives National Museum**: The Maldives National Museum in Male, the capital city, is a great place to learn about the country's history, culture, and traditions. The museum houses several artifacts, including traditional costumes, weapons, and household items.

**Traditional Games**: Maldivians have several traditional games, including a form of hopscotch called Haali Pittoo and a game similar to tag called Kulhi Fathi. These games are often played during festivals and gatherings.

**Maldivian Art**: Maldivian art is heavily influenced by Islamic calligraphy and geometric designs. Traditional art forms include lacquer work, mat weaving, and wooden carvings.

**Cultural Etiquette**: Maldivians value respect and politeness. It is customary to greet people with a smile and a nod, and to use formal titles when addressing elders or people in positions of authority. Pointing with the finger is considered rude, and it is polite to use the whole hand.

**Coconut**: The coconut is a staple in Maldivian cuisine and culture. Every part of the coconut is used, from the water to the meat and the oil. It is also used in traditional medicine and beauty treatments.

**Traditional Medicinal Practices**: Maldivians use several plants and herbs for medicinal purposes, such as ginger for colds and coughs and lemongrass for fever and stomach problems. These traditional remedies are passed down from generation to generation.

**Fishing**: Fishing has been a significant part of Maldivian culture for centuries. The country's economy relies heavily on fishing, and it is an essential source of food for the locals.

**Coral Stone Mosques**: The Maldives is home to several beautiful coral stone mosques, which are a unique feature of Islamic architecture in the country. The Hukuru Miskiy mosque in Male is a UNESCO World Heritage Site.

**Women's Dress**: Women in Maldives wear a dress called the libaas, which is made of lightweight fabric and is worn with a headscarf. The dress covers the body from the shoulders to the ankles, and it is often brightly colored and embroidered.

**Folklore**: Maldives has several folktales and legends that have been passed down through generations. These stories often feature mythical creatures such as water spirits and sea monsters.

**Traditional Boat Building**: The Maldives has a rich tradition of boat building, and the country's wooden dhoni boats are known for their durability and craftsmanship. The boats are still used for fishing and transportation today.

**Traditional Architecture**: Maldivian architecture is influenced by Islamic and South Asian styles. Traditional houses are made of coral stone and wood, and they feature intricate carvings and geometric patterns.

**Cultural Festivals**: Maldives celebrates several cultural festivals throughout the year, including Eid al-Fitr, Eid al-Adha, and the Islamic New Year. The country also celebrates National Day, Independence Day, and the Victory Day to commemorate the country's independence from British rule in 1965.

**Maldivian Cuisine**: Maldivian cuisine is a fusion of South Asian and Arabic influences, with an emphasis on seafood and coconut-based dishes. Some popular dishes include mas huni (a breakfast dish made of smoked tuna, grated coconut, and onions), garudhiya (a fish broth served with rice), and boshi mashuni (a salad made of dried tuna, grated coconut, and chili).

**Traditional Crafts**: Maldives is known for its traditional crafts, such as lacquer work, mat weaving, and wooden carvings. These crafts are often passed down from generation to generation and are an important part of the country's cultural heritage.

**Cultural Dress**: The traditional dress for men in Maldives is a sarong called the mundu, which is worn with a shirt. The mundu is made of cotton or silk and is often brightly colored. Women wear a dress called the libaas, which is also brightly colored and embroidered.

**Cultural Values**: Maldivians place a high value on community, family, and respect for elders. Hospitality is also an essential aspect of the culture, and guests are often welcomed with open arms and treated with generosity and kindness.

**Traditional Sports**: Maldives has several traditional sports, such as baibala (a form of wrestling), farihi (a game similar to hockey), and bandiyaa (a game played with coconuts). These sports are often played during festivals and gatherings.

**Boduberu Music**: Boduberu music is a popular traditional Maldivian music form that is performed using drums, clapping, and singing. It has a distinct rhythm and beat that is often used in traditional dances.

**Island Culture**: Maldives is an archipelago of more than 1,000 islands, and each island has its unique culture and traditions. Island life is often centered around fishing and farming, and the community is tightly knit.

**Cultural Dances**: Maldives has several traditional dances, such as the bandiya dance (performed with coconuts), the langiri dance (performed by women), and the thaareshey (performed during weddings).

**Cultural Heritage Sites**: The Maldives has several cultural heritage sites, including the Maldives National Museum, the Hukuru Miskiy mosque, and the Utheemu Ganduvaru (a historic residence of a former Maldivian sultan). These sites provide insight into the country's rich history and cultural heritage.

**Dhivehi Language**: The official language of Maldives is Dhivehi, which is spoken by the majority of the population. The language has its own unique script and is closely related to Sinhala, which is spoken in Sri Lanka.

**Islam**: Islam is the official religion of Maldives, and the majority of the population follows the Sunni branch of Islam. The country's legal system is based on Islamic law, and the call to prayer can be heard five times a day.

**Traditional Medicine**: Maldives has a long history of traditional medicine, which is based on natural remedies and practices. Traditional healers, known as fanditha, use a combination of herbs, massages, and incantations to treat various ailments.

**Dhoni**: The dhoni is a traditional Maldivian boat that has been used for centuries for fishing and transportation. The boats are made of coconut timber and are often brightly painted with intricate designs.

**Coral Stone Architecture**: Many of the buildings in Maldives are constructed using coral stone, which is a local material that is abundant in the region. The buildings feature intricate carvings and designs, and are often painted in bright colors.

**Maldivian Folktales**: Maldives has a rich tradition of storytelling, and many of the folktales feature mythical creatures and heroes. The stories are often passed down orally and provide insight into the country's cultural beliefs and values.

**Coconut Palm**: The coconut palm is an essential part of Maldivian culture and is used for a variety of purposes, including food, drink, and building materials. The tree is also considered sacred and is often used in religious ceremonies.

**Traditional Fishing**: Fishing is a vital part of Maldives culture, and traditional fishing methods are still used today. Fishermen use hand lines and nets to catch fish, and the catch is often sold at local markets.

**Cultural Etiquette**: Maldivians place a high value on respect and hospitality, and it is important to be mindful of cultural etiquette when visiting the country. For example, it is customary to remove shoes before entering a mosque or someone's home, and it is considered impolite to touch someone's head.

**Cultural Preservation**: Maldives places a high value on preserving its cultural heritage, and the government has implemented several initiatives to protect and promote traditional practices and customs. This includes funding for cultural events and festivals, as well as efforts to preserve historic sites and traditional crafts.

## Maldives top Hotels

The Maldives is a tropical paradise consisting of over 1,000 coral islands scattered across the Indian Ocean. The stunning natural beauty of the Maldives attracts visitors from all over the world, and the country is known for its luxurious resorts and hotels. Here are some of the top hotels in the Maldives:

**1. Soneva Fushi**: This eco-friendly resort is located on the Baa Atoll and features luxurious villas with private pools and outdoor bathrooms. Guests can enjoy a range of activities, including snorkeling, diving, and stargazing.

While the exact experience may vary depending on your preferences and the activities you choose, here is a general idea of what you can expect during a typical day at Soneva Fushi:

Wake up in your spacious and beautifully appointed villa, which may be set among the trees or on the beachfront. Enjoy a cup of coffee or tea on your private deck, taking in the ocean or jungle views.

Head to the resort's main dining area for breakfast, where you can enjoy a wide selection of fresh and healthy options, including fruits, juices, pastries, and made-to-order dishes.

Spend the morning relaxing on the beach, lounging by the pool, or exploring the island's natural beauty. You may want to take a guided nature walk, go snorkeling or diving, or try your hand at paddle boarding or kayaking.

For lunch, you can choose from several dining options, including a beachfront barbecue, a picnic on a deserted island, or a gourmet meal in one of the resort's restaurants.

In the afternoon, you may want to visit the spa for a relaxing massage or other wellness treatment, or take part in a yoga or meditation session. Alternatively, you can explore the island's cultural offerings, such as a visit to the local village or a cooking class.

As the day winds down, head to the resort's main bar for a pre-dinner cocktail, or enjoy a private dinner on your villa's deck or in a secluded beach location. The resort offers a variety of dining experiences, including Japanese, Mediterranean, and seafood cuisine, as well as private dining options.

After dinner, you can enjoy a nightcap at the bar, stargaze from your villa's deck, or take a night snorkeling tour to see the island's nocturnal marine life.

During the night, Soneva Fushi offers a tranquil and luxurious atmosphere for guests to unwind and enjoy the natural beauty of the Maldives. Here are some things you can expect during the night at Soneva Fushi:

Relaxing in your villa: Each villa at Soneva Fushi is designed to provide maximum comfort and privacy. You can unwind in your own private pool, gaze up at the stars from your rooftop terrace, or enjoy a movie in your in-villa cinema.

Fine dining: Soneva Fushi offers a range of dining experiences, from intimate private dinners to gourmet meals in one of the resort's restaurants. You can savor fresh seafood, Japanese cuisine, or Mediterranean-inspired dishes, all prepared with locally sourced ingredients.

Stargazing: The Maldives is known for its clear skies, making it an ideal destination for stargazing. Soneva Fushi offers a dedicated observatory with state-of-the-art telescopes, where you can learn about the constellations and marvel at the stars.

Night snorkeling: The marine life in the Maldives is just as fascinating at night as it is during the day. Soneva Fushi offers guided night snorkeling tours, where you can observe nocturnal creatures such as squid, lobsters, and octopuses.

Entertainment: Soneva Fushi often hosts live music, cultural performances, and other events for guests to enjoy. You can also relax at the resort's bars, sipping on cocktails and soaking up the island vibes.

Spa treatments: The resort's spa offers a range of wellness treatments designed to relax and rejuvenate your body and mind. You can indulge in a massage, body scrub, or facial, all using natural and organic products.

Overall, a day at Soneva Fushi is all about relaxation, rejuvenation, and immersion in the natural beauty of the Maldives. Whether you prefer adventure or pampering, the resort offers something for everyone.

**2. Six Senses Laamu**: Situated on a remote island in the southern part of the Maldives, Six Senses Laamu offers guests a unique and unforgettable experience. The resort has overwater villas, beach villas, and treehouse villas, all of which are designed to blend seamlessly with the natural surroundings.

Here is what you can expect during a typical day at Six Senses Laamu:

Wake up in your luxurious villa, which is nestled in the tropical vegetation or situated over the lagoon. Enjoy a cup of coffee or tea on your private deck, taking in the stunning views of the ocean or the lush island foliage.

Head to the resort's main restaurant for breakfast, where you can enjoy a range of fresh and healthy options, including local fruits, pastries, and made-to-order dishes.

Spend the morning exploring the island's natural beauty, either on land or in the water. You may want to take a guided snorkeling tour, go kayaking or paddleboarding, or take a yoga or meditation class.

For lunch, you can choose from a range of dining options, including a beach picnic, a seafood barbecue, or a gourmet meal in one of the resort's restaurants.

In the afternoon, you can indulge in a spa treatment or enjoy a relaxing swim in the pool. Alternatively, you may want to take a cooking class or visit a local village to learn about Maldivian culture.

As the day winds down, head to the resort's bar for a pre-dinner cocktail, or enjoy a private dinner on the beach or in your villa. The resort offers a range of dining experiences, including Japanese, Mediterranean, and Maldivian cuisine.

After dinner, you can enjoy a nightcap at the bar, go stargazing, or take a night fishing tour to catch your own dinner.

Here are some things you can expect during the night at Six Senses Laamu:

Fine dining: The resort's restaurants offer a range of gourmet dining options, including seafood, international cuisine, and local Maldivian dishes. You can enjoy a romantic dinner under the stars or a private dining experience in your villa.

Night snorkeling: The resort's house reef is just as beautiful at night as it is during the day. You can take a guided night snorkeling tour to observe the nocturnal marine life, including bioluminescent plankton and reef sharks.

Cinema under the stars: The resort offers a unique cinema experience, where you can watch your favorite movie under the stars while lounging on comfortable beanbags and sipping on cocktails.

Live entertainment: Six Senses Laamu often hosts live music and cultural performances for guests to enjoy. You can relax at the resort's bar while listening to local musicians or watching traditional Maldivian dance performances.

Stargazing: The Maldives is known for its clear skies, making it an ideal destination for stargazing. The resort offers a stargazing experience, where you can learn about the constellations and marvel at the stars.

Night fishing: You can try your hand at night fishing, a traditional Maldivian activity where you can catch your own dinner and have it cooked by the resort's chefs.

Private in-villa experiences: If you prefer a more intimate experience, the resort offers a range of in-villa experiences, including private dining, spa treatments, and movies.

**3. St. Regis Maldives Vommuli Resort**: Located on a private island in the Dhaalu Atoll, the St. Regis Maldives Vommuli Resort offers guests unparalleled luxury and comfort. The resort features overwater villas, beach villas, and a range of dining options.

Here is what you can expect during a typical day at St. Regis Maldives Vommuli Resort:

Wake up in your overwater villa, which features stunning views of the Indian Ocean and direct access to the turquoise waters. Enjoy a cup of coffee or tea on your private deck or take a dip in your private pool.

Head to the resort's main restaurant for breakfast, where you can enjoy a variety of international and local cuisine, including freshly baked bread, tropical fruits, and made-to-order dishes.

Spend the morning exploring the island's natural beauty. You may want to take a guided snorkeling tour, go kayaking or paddleboarding, or take a yoga or meditation class.

For lunch, you can choose from a range of dining options, including a beach picnic, a seafood barbecue, or a gourmet meal in one of the resort's restaurants.

In the afternoon, you can indulge in a spa treatment or relax by the infinity pool while taking in the stunning ocean views. Alternatively, you may want to take a cooking class or visit a local village to learn about Maldivian culture.

As the day winds down, head to the resort's bar for a pre-dinner cocktail or enjoy a private dinner on the beach or in your villa. The resort offers a range of dining experiences, including Italian, Asian, and Maldivian cuisine.

After dinner, you can enjoy a nightcap at the bar, go stargazing, or take a night fishing tour to catch your own dinner.

During the night, the St. Regis Maldives Vommuli Resort offers a variety of experiences and activities for guests to enjoy. Here are some things you can expect during the night at St. Regis Maldives Vommuli Resort:

Fine dining: The resort's restaurants offer a range of gourmet dining options, including seafood, international cuisine, and Maldivian dishes. You can enjoy a romantic dinner under the stars or a private dining experience in your villa.

Sunset cocktails: The resort offers a range of bars and lounges where you can enjoy cocktails and light bites while taking in the stunning sunset over the Indian Ocean.

Nighttime spa treatments: The resort's spa offers a range of nighttime treatments, including massages, facials, and aromatherapy sessions. You can indulge in a relaxing spa experience under the stars.

Nighttime beach walks: Take a peaceful stroll along the beach at night, listening to the sound of the waves and feeling the warm ocean breeze.

Cinema under the stars: The resort offers a unique cinema experience, where you can watch your favorite movie under the stars while lounging on comfortable beanbags and sipping on cocktails.

Nighttime fishing: You can try your hand at night fishing, a traditional Maldivian activity where you can catch your own dinner and have it cooked by the resort's chefs.

Stargazing: The Maldives is known for its clear skies, making it an ideal destination for stargazing. The resort offers a stargazing experience, where you can learn about the constellations and marvel at the stars.

**4. Four Seasons Resort Maldives at Landaa Giraavaru**: This luxury resort is located in the Baa Atoll and offers guests a range of activities, including diving, snorkeling, and surfing. The resort also features an award-winning spa and a variety of dining options.

Here is what you can expect during a typical day at the resort:

Wake up in your spacious villa, which features a private pool and stunning views of the turquoise waters of the Indian Ocean. Enjoy a cup of coffee or tea on your private deck or take a dip in your pool.

Head to the resort's main restaurant for breakfast, where you can enjoy a variety of international and local cuisine, including fresh fruit, pastries, and made-to-order dishes.

Spend the morning exploring the island's natural beauty. You can go snorkeling in the coral reefs, take a guided nature walk through the island's lush vegetation, or relax on the beach and soak up the sun.

For lunch, you can choose from a range of dining options, including a beach barbecue, a sushi lunch, or a gourmet meal in one of the resort's restaurants.

In the afternoon, you can indulge in a spa treatment or take part in one of the resort's many activities, such as yoga, Pilates, or a cooking class. You can also go on a dolphin watching tour or take a boat trip to explore nearby islands.

As the day winds down, head to the resort's bar for a pre-dinner cocktail or enjoy a private dinner on the beach or in your villa. The resort offers a range of dining experiences, including Japanese, Italian, and Maldivian cuisine.

After dinner, you can enjoy a nightcap at the bar or take a romantic stroll on the beach under the starry night sky.

During the night, the Four Seasons Resort Maldives at Landaa Giraavaru offers a range of activities and experiences for guests to enjoy. Here are some things you can expect during the night at the resort:

Fine dining: The resort's restaurants offer a range of gourmet dining options, including seafood, international cuisine, and Maldivian dishes. You can enjoy a romantic dinner under the stars or a private dining experience in your villa.

Stargazing: The Maldives is known for its clear skies, making it an ideal destination for stargazing. The resort offers a stargazing experience, where you can learn about the constellations and marvel at the stars.

Nighttime spa treatments: The resort's spa offers a range of nighttime treatments, including massages, facials, and aromatherapy sessions. You can indulge in a relaxing spa experience under the stars.

Nighttime beach walks: Take a peaceful stroll along the beach at night, listening to the sound of the waves and feeling the warm ocean breeze.

Sunset cocktails: The resort offers a range of bars and lounges where you can enjoy cocktails and light bites while taking in the stunning sunset over the Indian Ocean.

Night fishing: You can try your hand at night fishing, a traditional Maldivian activity where you can catch your own dinner and have it cooked by the resort's chefs.

Movie under the stars: The resort offers a unique cinema experience, where you can watch your favorite movie under the stars while lounging on comfortable beanbags and sipping on cocktails.

**5. One&Only Reethi Rah**: This resort is located on one of the largest islands in the North Malé Atoll and features 130 private villas, including overwater villas and beach villas. The resort offers a range of activities, including water sports, tennis, and yoga.

**6. Cheval Blanc Randheli**: This ultra-luxury resort is located on a private island in the Noonu Atoll and offers guests spacious villas with private pools and butler service.

**7. COMO Cocoa Island**: This boutique resort is located on a small private island in the South Malé Atoll and features overwater villas that are designed to resemble traditional Maldivian fishing boats.

**8. Gili Lankanfushi**: This eco-friendly resort is located on a private island in the North Malé Atoll and offers guests spacious overwater villas with private decks and direct access to the crystal-clear waters below.

**9. Velaa Private Island**: This ultra-luxury resort is located on a private island in the Noonu Atoll and offers guests a range of activities, including golf, tennis, and watersports.

**10. Anantara Kihavah Maldives Villas**: This luxurious resort is located in the Baa Atoll and features overwater villas with private pools and direct access to the ocean.

Many of these hotels offer guests a range of activities, including snorkeling, diving, and other water sports. They also feature award-winning spas, gourmet restaurants, and other amenities designed to help guests relax and unwind.

## 10 top Beaches in Maldives

The Maldives is famous for its pristine beaches and crystal-clear waters, making it a popular destination for tourists all around the world. Here are ten of the top beaches in the Maldives:

**1. Veligandu Island Beach**: Located in the North Ari Atoll, Veligandu Island Beach is one of the most beautiful beaches in the Maldives. The powdery white sand and crystal-clear waters make it a perfect spot for swimming and sunbathing.

**2. Bikini Beach**: As the name suggests, Bikini Beach is a great place to soak up some sun in your swimsuit. Located in Maafushi, Bikini Beach is a public beach that offers visitors a chance to relax and unwind in a beautiful setting.

**3. Fulhadhoo Beach**: Fulhadhoo Beach is a remote beach on Fulhadhoo Island, located in Baa Atoll. The beach is known for its calm waters and white sand, making it a perfect place for swimming and snorkeling.

**4. Nalaguraidhoo Beach**: Nalaguraidhoo Beach is located on the island of Nalaguraidhoo in South Ari Atoll. The beach is known for its stunning coral reefs and underwater life, making it a popular spot for diving and snorkeling.

**5. Cocoa Island Beach**: Cocoa Island Beach is located in the South Male Atoll and is known for its beautiful white sand and clear blue waters. Visitors can enjoy water sports such as diving, snorkeling, and paddleboarding.

**6. Lily Beach**: Lily Beach is a luxurious private island resort located in the South Ari Atoll. The beach is known for its beautiful coral reefs, making it a popular spot for diving and snorkeling.

**7. Mirihi Island Beach**: Mirihi Island Beach is located in the South Ari Atoll and is known for its beautiful white sand and turquoise waters. Visitors can enjoy a range of water sports, including diving and snorkeling.

**8. Hulhumale Beach**: Hulhumale Beach is a man-made beach located in the island of Hulhumale. The beach is perfect for swimming and sunbathing, and visitors can also enjoy water sports such as surfing and kiteboarding.

**9. Reethi Beach**: Reethi Beach is a private island resort located in the Baa Atoll. The beach is known for its beautiful coral reefs and stunning sunsets, making it a perfect spot for romantic getaways.

**10. Vabbinfaru Island Beach**: Vabbinfaru Island Beach is located in the North Male Atoll and is known for its white sand and turquoise waters. Visitors can enjoy a range of water sports, including diving and snorkeling, and the beach is also a great spot for dolphin watching.

## Conclusion

In conclusion, Maldives is a breathtakingly beautiful destination that offers a truly unforgettable travel experience. From its stunning beaches and crystal-clear waters to its rich culture and traditions, Maldives is a true gem of the Indian Ocean. Whether you're looking to relax and unwind, explore the local culture and cuisine, or engage in thrilling water sports and activities, Maldives has something for everyone. With its warm and welcoming people, awe-inspiring natural beauty, and endless opportunities for adventure, Maldives is truly a traveler's paradise. So pack your bags, book your trip, and get ready for the journey of a lifetime in this magical island nation.

Printed in Great Britain
by Amazon